TABARRUJ
& ITS DANGERS

• SHAYKH ABDUL-AZĪZ BIN BĀZ رحمه الله •

© Qawlul Ahlil Ilm Publications, USA

All rights reserved. No part of this publication may be reproduced in any language, stored in any retrieval system, or transmitted in any form or by any means, whether electronic, mechanical, photocopying, recording, or otherwise, without the express permission of the copyright owner.

ISBN	:	978-1-7348143-4-7
First Edition	:	Safar, 1443 A.H. / September 2021 C.E.
Subject	:	Fiqh / Ahkaam
Cover Design	:	Aljadeed Design Co.
Translation by	:	Raha ibn Donald Batts
Website	:	www.qaipubs.com
Email	:	info@qaipubs.com

Table of Contents

Indecency and Its Dangers 7
The Danger of Women Sharing the Work Arena of Men . 25
The Ruling Regarding Intermingling While Studying 42
The Danger of Women Teaching Boys at the Primary School Level 55
Evil Affairs Which Must Be Avoided 59

Transliteration Table

Consonants

ء	ʾ	د	d	ض	ḍ	ك	k
ب	b	ذ	dh	ط	ṭ	ل	l
ت	t	ر	r	ظ	ẓ	م	m
ث	th	ز	z	ع	ʿ	ن	n
ج	j	س	s	غ	gh	ه	h
ح	ḥ	ش	sh	ف	f	و	w
خ	kh	ص	ṣ	ق	q	ي	y

Vowels

Short		َ	a	ِ	i	ُ	u
Long		ـَا	ā	ـِي	ī	ـُو	ū
Diphthongs		ـَي	ay	ـَو	aw		

Arabic Symbols & their meanings

عَزَّوَجَلَّ	سُبْحَانَهُ وَتَعَالَى	رَحِمَهُ ٱللَّهُ	حَفِظَهُ اللهُ
(Allāh) the Mighty & Sublime	Glorified & Exalted is Allāh	May Allāh have mercy on him	May Allāh preserve him

صَلَّى ٱللَّهُ عَلَيْهِ وَعَلَى آلِهِ وَسَلَّمَ	جَلَّ جَلَالُهُ	جَلَّ وَعَلَا	تَبَارَكَ وَتَعَالَى
May Allāh elevate his rank & grant him peace	(Allāh) His Majesty is Exalted	(Allāh) the Sublime & Exalted	(Allāh) the Blessed & Exalted

رَضِيَ ٱللَّهُ عَنْهُمْ	رَضِيَ ٱللَّهُ عَنْهَا	رَضِيَ ٱللَّهُ عَنْهُ	عَلَيْهِ ٱلصَّلَاةُ وَٱلسَّلَامُ
May Allāh be pleased with them	May Allāh be pleased with her	May Allāh be pleased with him	May Allāh elevate his rank & grant him peace

رَحِمَهُمُ ٱللَّهُ			
May Allāh have mercy upon them			

"In the name of Allah, most gracious and most merciful"

Indecency and Its Dangers

All the praise is for Allaah Alone; and may prayers and peace be upon he after whom there is no prophet, his family and companions. To proceed:

It is not hidden from anyone who has knowledge that which has swept many of the lands from At-Tabarruj on the part of many of the women and uncovering and revealing themselves to the men, as well as displaying much of their adornments which Allaah has prohibited them from displaying. Without doubt that is from the great evils and open acts of disobedience. It is likewise from the greatest reasons for the unleashing of punishment and the descending of inequities due to that which indecency and uncovering bring about from the appearance of lewdness, the committing of crimes, and the decrease of modesty. So have Taqwaa of Allaah, O Muslims, and control the foolish and prevent the women from that which Allaah has made prohibited for them and make them hold fast to the Hijaab and proper covering. Beware of the Anger of Allaah, the Glorified, and His Great Punishment.

It has been authentically reported from the Prophet (ﷺ) that he said:

»إِنَّ النَّاسَ إِذَا رَأَوْا الْمُنْكَرَ فَلَمْ يُنْكِرُوهُ أَوْشَكَ أَنْ يَعُمَّهُمْ اللَّهُ بِعِقَابِهِ«

"When the people see evil and do not change it then Allaah will cover them all with His punishment."

Allaah, the Glorified, said within His Noble Book:

﴿لُعِنَ ٱلَّذِينَ كَفَرُوا۟ مِنۢ بَنِىٓ إِسْرَٰٓءِيلَ عَلَىٰ لِسَانِ دَاوُۥدَ وَعِيسَى ٱبْنِ مَرْيَمَ ۚ ذَٰلِكَ بِمَا عَصَوا۟ وَّكَانُوا۟ يَعْتَدُونَ ۝ كَانُوا۟ لَا يَتَنَاهَوْنَ عَن مُّنكَرٍ فَعَلُوهُ ۚ لَبِئْسَ مَا كَانُوا۟ يَفْعَلُونَ ۝﴾

"Those among the Children of Israel who disbelieved were cursed by the tongue of Daawud (David) and 'Eesa (Jesus), son of Maryam (Mary). That was because they disobeyed (Allaah and the Messengers) and were ever transgressing beyond bounds. They used not to forbid one another from the Munkar (wrong, evildoing, sins, polytheism, disbelief, etc.) which they committed. Vile indeed was what they used to do." (Al-Ma'idah 5:78-79)

Within the Musnad and other book it is mentioned on the authority of Ibn Mas'ood (رضي الله عنه), that the Prophet (صلى الله عليه وسلم) recited this verse then said:

«وَالَّذِي نَفْسِي بِيَدِهِ لَتَأْمُرُنَّ بِالْمَعْرُوفِ، وَلَتَنْهَوُنَّ عَنِ الْمُنْكَرِ، وَلَتَأْخُذُنَّ عَلَى يَدِ السفيه، ولتأطرنَّه عَلَى الْحَقِّ أَطْرًا، أَوْ لَيَضْرِبَنَّ اللَّهُ قُلُوبَ بَعْضِكُمْ عَلَى بَعْضٍ، أَوْ ليلعَنْكم كَمَا لَعَنَهُمْ»

"By He in Whose Hand is my soul, you will enjoin the good, forbid the evil, grab hold of the hand of the foolish, and compel him to that which is correct or Allaah shall mix your hearts together and curse you just as He has cursed them."

It is likewise authentically reported from the Prophet (صلى الله عليه وسلم) that he said:

«مَنْ رَأَى مِنْكُمْ مُنْكَرًا فَلْيُغَيِّرْهُ بِيَدِهِ، فَإِنْ لَمْ يَسْتَطِعْ فَبِلِسَانِهِ، فَإِنْ لَمْ يَسْتَطِعْ فَبِقَلْبِهِ، وَذَلِكَ أَضْعَفُ الْإِيمَانِ»

"He from amongst you who sees an evil then let him change it with his hand; if he is not able, the with his tongue' if he is not able then with his heart, and that is the least of Eemaan."

Allaah, the Glorified, has commanded within His Noble Book, with the women covering themselves and remaining with their homes, and He warned against At-Tabarruj and being soft in speech to the men, as a means of protecting them from corruption and to warn them from the means of Fitnah. Allaah, Glorified and Exalted be He, said:

﴿يَٰنِسَآءَ ٱلنَّبِيِّ لَسۡتُنَّ كَأَحَدٖ مِّنَ ٱلنِّسَآءِ إِنِ ٱتَّقَيۡتُنَّ فَلَا تَخۡضَعۡنَ بِٱلۡقَوۡلِ فَيَطۡمَعَ ٱلَّذِي فِي قَلۡبِهِۦ مَرَضٞ وَقُلۡنَ قَوۡلٗا مَّعۡرُوفٗا ۝ وَقَرۡنَ فِي بُيُوتِكُنَّ وَلَا تَبَرَّجۡنَ تَبَرُّجَ ٱلۡجَٰهِلِيَّةِ ٱلۡأُولَىٰۖ وَأَقِمۡنَ ٱلصَّلَوٰةَ وَءَاتِينَ ٱلزَّكَوٰةَ وَأَطِعۡنَ ٱللَّهَ وَرَسُولَهُۥٓ﴾

"O wives of the Prophet! You are not like any other women. If you keep your duty (to Allaah), then be not soft in speech, lest he in whose heart is a disease (of hypocrisy, or evil desire for adultery, etc.) should be moved with desire, but speak in an honorable manner. And stay in your houses, and do not display yourselves like that of the times of ignorance, and perform As-Salat, and give Zakat and obey Allaah and His Messenger." (Al-Ahzab 33:32-33)

Within these verses Allaah has prohibited the wives of the Noble Prophet, the mothers of the believers—who are the best of the women and the purest of them—from being soft in speech with the men; which is to be mild and inviting in speech, in order that he in whose heart there is a disease would not be moved with desire for fornication and think that they are in agreement with him regarding that. He likewise commanded them to stay within their homes and he prohibited them from the indecency of pre-Islamic ignorance. This is to display their adornments and beauty; such as (showing) the head, the face, the neck, the chest, the arms, the legs, and the likes of that, due to that which this contains from great corruption and Fitnah as well as moving the hearts of the men towards to means which lead to fornication. If Allaah warned the mothers of the believers from these evil things—with their (level) of righteousness, Eemaan, and purity, then other than them are more (in need of being prohibited), and more in need of being warned, rebuked, and (reminded) to fear the causes of Fitnah. May Allaah protect us and all of the Muslims from the causes of Fitnah.

That which proves that the ruling is general—for them as well as other than them—is the statement of Allaah, the Exalted, within his verse:

﴿ وَأَقِمْنَ ٱلصَّلَوٰةَ وَءَاتِينَ ٱلزَّكَوٰةَ وَأَطِعْنَ ٱللَّهَ وَرَسُولَهُۥٓ ﴾

"And perform As-Salat, and give Zakat and obey Allaah and His Messenger." (Al-Ahzab 33:33)

These commands are general rulings, for the wives of the Prophet (ﷺ) as well as other than them.

Allaah, the Mighty and Majestic, said:

﴿ وَإِذَا سَأَلْتُمُوهُنَّ مَتَٰعًا فَسْـَٔلُوهُنَّ مِن وَرَآءِ حِجَابٍ ۚ ذَٰلِكُمْ أَطْهَرُ لِقُلُوبِكُمْ وَقُلُوبِهِنَّ ﴾

"And when you ask (his wives) for anything you want, ask them from behind a screen, that is purer for your hearts and for their hearts." (Al-Ahzab 33:53)

This noble verse is a clear text regarding the obligation of the women wearing Hijaab (veiling and) covering themselves from the men. Allaah has clarified within this verse that veiling is purer for the hearts of the men as well as the women and further from lewdness and its means. He, likewise, indicated that uncovering and not wearing Hijaab if filthy and impure whereas wearing it is purity and safety.

So assembly of Muslims, have good manners with Allaah and adhere to the command of Allaah. Make the Hijaab—which is a cause for purity and means for safety—binding upon your womenfolk.

Allaah, the Glorified and High, has said:

﴿ يَٰٓأَيُّهَا ٱلنَّبِىُّ قُل لِّأَزْوَٰجِكَ وَبَنَاتِكَ وَنِسَآءِ ٱلْمُؤْمِنِينَ يُدْنِينَ عَلَيْهِنَّ مِن جَلَٰبِيبِهِنَّ ۚ ذَٰلِكَ أَدْنَىٰٓ أَن يُعْرَفْنَ فَلَا يُؤْذَيْنَ ۗ وَكَانَ ٱللَّهُ غَفُورًا رَّحِيمًا ۝ ﴾

"O Prophet! Tell your wives and your daughters and the women of the believers to draw their cloaks (veils) all over their bodies (i.e., screen themselves completely except the eyes or one eye to see the way). That will be better, that they should be known (as free respectable women) so as not to be annoyed.

And Allaah is Ever Oft-Forgiving, Most Merciful." (Al-Ahzab 33:59)

The word Al-Jalaabeeb is the plural of Jilbaab; and it is that which the woman puts on over her head and body above the clothing in order that she may cover herself therewith. Allaah commanded all believing women to outwardly display their Jalabeeb over their beauty; from their hair, face, and other than that in order that they may be known to have chastity and that they should not be put to trial nor should they put others to trial and thus they should be harmed. 'Alee ibn Aboo Talhah (رحمه الله) reported from Ibn 'Abbaas (رضي الله عنه) that he said: **"Allaah commanded the believing women that when they leave their homes for a need that they cover their faces from above their heads with the Jalaabeeb, and to display one eye."** Muhammad ibn Seereen said: "I asked 'Ubaydah As-Salmaanee about the statement of Allaah, the Mighty and Majestic:

﴿يُدْنِينَ عَلَيْهِنَّ مِن جَلَٰبِيبِهِنَّ﴾

"Tell your wives and your daughters and the women of the believers to draw their cloaks (veils) all over their bodies." (Al-Ahzab 33:59)

He covered his face and head leaving out his eye (to illustrate)."

Moreover, Allaah informed that He is the Oft-Forgiving and the Most Merciful regarding that which has preceded from shortcomings in that before the prohibition and warning came.

Allaah, the Mighty and Majestic said:

Indecency and Its Dangers | 13

﴿وَٱلْقَوَاعِدُ مِنَ ٱلنِّسَاءِ ٱلَّٰتِي لَا يَرْجُونَ نِكَاحًا فَلَيْسَ عَلَيْهِنَّ جُنَاحٌ أَن يَضَعْنَ ثِيَابَهُنَّ غَيْرَ مُتَبَرِّجَٰتٍۭ بِزِينَةٍۢ ۖ وَأَن يَسْتَعْفِفْنَ خَيْرٌۭ لَّهُنَّ ۗ وَٱللَّهُ سَمِيعٌ عَلِيمٌ ۝﴾

"And as for women past child-bearing who do not expect wed-lock, it is no sin on them if they discard their (outer) clothing in such a way as not to show their adornment. But to refrain (i.e. not to discard their outer clothing) is better for them. And Allaah is All-Hearer, All-Knower." (An-Nur 24:60)

Allaah informs that those women who are past child-bearing age—who are the elder women that do not expect marriage—there is no harm upon them if they uncover their faces and hands if they are indecently displaying their beauty. By way of this it is known that the woman who indecently displays her beauty is not allowed to discard her garment, uncovering her face, hands, and other than that from her adornments. And it is upon her to cover these things even if she is an elder. This is because for everything that is lost there is one who will find it (i.e., although this rule doesn't apply to some there are some that is does apply to. Also, because At-Tabarruj leads to Fitnah on the part of the indecently clad woman, even if she may be older. So how about the young and beautiful lady when she indecently exposes herself? Without doubt her sin is greater, the blame upon her is worse, and the Fitnah is more severe.

Allaah set as a condition, as it relates to the elder woman, that she does not expect marriage. This is not except due to—and Allaah knows best—the fact that her hope for marriage would compel her to beautify herself and display her adornments out of desire for potential suitors. Therefore, she has been prohibited to from discarding her covering and showing her beauty as a means of protection for her and other than her from Fitnah. Then He completed the verse with the encouragement those who do not expect marriage toward chastity and He clarified that it is better for them even though they would not be indecently exposing themselves if they didn't. By way of this the virtue of veiling and covering oneself with one's garments—even for the elderly—becomes clear; and the fact that it is better for them than discarding their covering. Therefore, this necessitates that veiling and chastity; refraining from displaying adornments is better and more binding upon the younger ladies and further from Fitnah for them. Allaah said:

﴿قُل لِّلْمُؤْمِنِينَ يَغُضُّوا مِنْ أَبْصَٰرِهِمْ وَيَحْفَظُوا فُرُوجَهُمْ ذَٰلِكَ أَزْكَىٰ لَهُمْ إِنَّ ٱللَّهَ خَبِيرٌۢ بِمَا يَصْنَعُونَ ۝ وَقُل لِّلْمُؤْمِنَٰتِ يَغْضُضْنَ مِنْ أَبْصَٰرِهِنَّ وَيَحْفَظْنَ فُرُوجَهُنَّ وَلَا يُبْدِينَ زِينَتَهُنَّ إِلَّا مَا ظَهَرَ مِنْهَا وَلْيَضْرِبْنَ بِخُمُرِهِنَّ عَلَىٰ جُيُوبِهِنَّ وَلَا يُبْدِينَ زِينَتَهُنَّ إِلَّا لِبُعُولَتِهِنَّ أَوْ ءَابَآئِهِنَّ أَوْ ءَابَآءِ بُعُولَتِهِنَّ أَوْ أَبْنَآئِهِنَّ أَوْ أَبْنَآءِ بُعُولَتِهِنَّ أَوْ إِخْوَٰنِهِنَّ أَوْ بَنِىٓ إِخْوَٰنِهِنَّ أَوْ بَنِىٓ أَخَوَٰتِهِنَّ أَوْ نِسَآئِهِنَّ أَوْ مَا مَلَكَتْ أَيْمَٰنُهُنَّ أَوِ ٱلتَّٰبِعِينَ غَيْرِ أُو۟لِى ٱلْإِرْبَةِ مِنَ ٱلرِّجَالِ أَوِ ٱلطِّفْلِ ٱلَّذِينَ لَمْ يَظْهَرُوا عَلَىٰ عَوْرَٰتِ ٱلنِّسَآءِ وَلَا يَضْرِبْنَ بِأَرْجُلِهِنَّ لِيُعْلَمَ مَا يُخْفِينَ مِن زِينَتِهِنَّ وَتُوبُوٓا۟ إِلَى ٱللَّهِ جَمِيعًا أَيُّهَ ٱلْمُؤْمِنُونَ لَعَلَّكُمْ تُفْلِحُونَ ۝﴾

"Tell the believing men to lower their gaze (from looking at forbidden things), and protect their private parts (from illegal sexual acts, etc.). That is purer for them. Verily, Allaah is All-Aware of what they do. And tell the believing women to lower their gaze (from looking at forbidden things), and protect their private parts (from illegal sexual acts, etc.) and not to show off their adornment except only that which is apparent; and to draw their veils all over Juyubihinna (i.e. their bodies, faces, necks and bosoms, etc.) and not to reveal their adornment except to their husbands, their fathers, their husband's fathers, their sons, their husband's sons, their brothers or their brother's sons, or their sister's sons, or their (Muslim) women (i.e. their sisters in Islâm), or the (female) slaves whom their right hands possess, or old male servants who lack vigor, or small children who have no sense of the shame of sex. And let them not stamp their feet so as to reveal what they hide of their adornment. And all of you beg Allaah to forgive you all, O believers, that you may be successful." (An-Nur 24:30-31)

Within these two verses Allaah commands the believing men and women to lower their gaze and to preserve their private parts. This is not except due to the heinousness of lewd fornication and that which it brings about from great corruption between the Muslims. Also, because allowing the eyes to roam freely is from the means which lead to diseases of the heart and falling into lewd acts whereas lowering the gaze is from the means to safety from that. Due to this, Allaah (سُبْحَانَهُ وَتَعَالَى) said:

$$\text{﴿ قُل لِّلْمُؤْمِنِينَ يَغُضُّوا۟ مِنْ أَبْصَٰرِهِمْ وَيَحْفَظُوا۟ فُرُوجَهُمْ ۚ ذَٰلِكَ أَزْكَىٰ لَهُمْ ۗ إِنَّ ٱللَّهَ خَبِيرٌۢ بِمَا يَصْنَعُونَ ﴾}$$

"Tell the believing men to lower their gaze (from looking at forbidden things), and protect their private parts (from illegal sexual acts, etc.). That is purer for them. Verily, Allaah is All-Aware of what they do." (An-Nur 24:30)

Lowering the gaze and safeguarding the private parts are purer for the believer in the Dunyaa and the hereafter, whereas allowing them to roam freely is from the greatest means of destruction and punishment in the Dunyaa and the hereafter. We ask Allaah for safety from that.

Allaah, the Mighty and Majestic, informed that He is All-Aware of what the people do and that nothing is hidden from Him. In this lies a warning to the believer from committing that which Allaah has prohibited and turning away from that which Allaah has legislated. It is also a reminder for him that Allaah, the Glorified, sees him and knows his actions, whether good or bad. As He said:

$$\text{﴿ يَعْلَمُ خَائِنَةَ ٱلْأَعْيُنِ وَمَا تُخْفِى ٱلصُّدُورُ ﴾}$$

"Allaah knows the fraud of the eyes, and all that the breasts conceal." (Ghafir 40:19)

Likewise, he (سُبْحَانَهُ وَتَعَالَى) said:

$$\text{﴿ وَمَا تَكُونُ فِى شَأْنٍ وَمَا تَتْلُوا۟ مِنْهُ مِن قُرْءَانٍ وَلَا تَعْمَلُونَ مِنْ عَمَلٍ إِلَّا كُنَّا عَلَيْكُمْ شُهُودًا إِذْ تُفِيضُونَ فِيهِ ﴾}$$

"Whatever you (O Muhammad) may be doing, and whatever portion you may be reciting from the

Indecency and Its Dangers | 17

Qur'aan, - and whatever deed you (mankind) may be doing (good or evil), We are Witness thereof, when you are doing it." (Yunus 10:61)

Therefore, it is obligatory upon the slave to beware of his Lord and to be shy before Him that He should see him disobeying Him or neglecting being obedient to Him in that which he has made obligatory upon him.

He (سُبْحَانَهُ وَتَعَالَى) then said:

﴿وَقُل لِّلْمُؤْمِنَٰتِ يَغْضُضْنَ مِنْ أَبْصَٰرِهِنَّ وَيَحْفَظْنَ فُرُوجَهُنَّ﴾

"And tell the believing women to lower their gaze (from looking at forbidden things), and protect their private parts."

He commanded the believing women to lower their gaze and to safeguard their private parts, just as He commanded the believing men; this is for the purpose of protecting them from the means to Fitnah and as an encouragement for them to the means which lead to chastity and safety. Then He (سُبْحَانَهُ وَتَعَالَى) said:

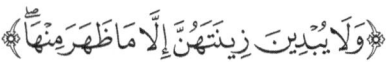

"And not to show off their adornment except only that which is apparent"

Ibn Mas'ood (رَضِيَ اللَّهُ عَنْهُ) said: **"That which is apparent from it, means that which is apparent from their garments. That is pardoned."** His intent here is the clothing that does not contain At-Tabarruj and Fitnah. As for that which was reported by Ibn Abbaas (رَضِيَ اللَّهُ عَنْهُ), that he explained: That which is apparent from it, to be the face and hands then this is interpreted to be the state of the women before the verse of veiling was revealed. As for after that then it Allaah made it obligatory upon them to cover everything, as has preceded within the noble verses from Soorah Al-Ahzaab and other than it. What proves that Ibn 'Abbaas (رضي الله عنه) intended this is that which 'Alee ibn Aboo Talhah (رحمه الله) that he said: **"Allaah has commanded the believing women to cover their faces from above their heads with their Jalaabeeb and to only display one eye."** Shaykhul-Islaam Ibn Taymiyah (رحمه الله) and others from the people of knowledge and verification have stated that this is the Haqq in which there is no doubt.

It is known that which the women displaying the face and hands brings about from corruption and Fitnah. The statement of Allaah has previously been mentioned:

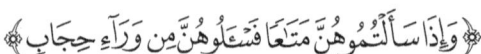

"And when you ask (his wives) for anything you want, ask them from behind a screen."
(Al-Ahzab 33:53)

He made no exceptions. This is a decisive verse. Therefore, it is obligatory to adopt it and to implement it and to interpret anything else in light of it. This ruling is general, regarding the wives of the Prophet (صلى الله عليه وسلم) as well as other than them from the believing women. There has been previously mentioned from Soorah An-Noor that which indicates that. It is that which Allaah mentioned as it relates to those who do not expect marriage and the prohibition of them discarding their garments except with two conditions.

1. They do not expect marriage.
2. They do not do so being indecently showing off their adornments.

Speech has been previously mentioned regarding that. They aforementioned verse is a clear proof and a decisive evidence for the prohibition of the women uncovering and indecently displaying their beauty.

This is also proven by that which is affirmed on the authority of 'Aa'ishah (رضي الله عنها), in the story of the slander wherein she covered her face when she heard the voice of Safwaan ibn Al-Mu'attal As-Sulamee (رضي الله عنه), and she said that he used to know her before the Hijaab. This proves that after the revelation of the verse of the Hijaab, the women were not identified, due to them veiling and covering their faces. That which the women have fallen into today, from going great lengths in At-Tabarruj and displaying their beauty is not hidden. Hence, it is obligatory to block the means which lead to corruption and lewdness.

From the greatest of the means to corruption is men being secluded with the women and traveling with them without a Mahram. It has been authentically reported from the Prophet (صلى الله عليه وسلم) that he said:

«لَا تُسَافِرِ الْمَرْأَةُ إِلَّا مَعَ ذِي مَحْرَمٍ، وَلَا يَخْلُوَنَّ رَجُلٌ بِامْرَأَةٍ إِلَّا وَمَعَهَا ذُو مَحْرَمٍ»

"A woman is not to travel except with a Mahram and a man is not to be secluded with a woman unless there is a Mahram with her."

He (ﷺ) likewise said:

«لَا يَخْلُوَنَّ رَجُلٌ بِامْرَأَةٍ إِلَّا كَانَ ثالِثَهما الشَّيْطَان»

"A man is not secluded with a woman except that Shaytaan is their third party."

He (ﷺ) also said:

«لَا يَبِيتَنَّ رَجُلٌ عِنْدَ امْرَأَةٍ، إِلَّا أَنْ يَكُونَ نَاكِحًا، أَوْ ذَا مَحْرَمٍ»

"A man is not to spend the night alone with a woman unless he is a husband or relative of hers." (Reported by Muslim within his Saheeh)

Therefore, have Taqwaa of Allaah, O Muslims, and control your womenfolk. Prevent them from that which Allaah has made prohibited, from uncovering, indecency, and displaying their beauty and imitation of the enemies of Allaah, from the Christians and those like them. And know that silence regarding them is sharing with them in the sin and exposing oneself to the Wrath of Allaah and His all-encompassing punishment. May Allaah protect us and you from the evil of that.

From the greatest of obligations is warning men from being secluded with women, entering upon them, and traveling with them without a Mahram. This is because that is from the means to Fitnah and corruption. It has been authentically narrated form the Prophet (ﷺ) that he said:

«مَا تَرَكْتُ بَعْدِي فِتْنَةً أَضَرَّ عَلَى الرِّجَالِ مِنَ النِّسَاءِ»

"I have left no greater Fitnah behind for the men than the women."

He (ﷺ) likewise said:

«إِنَّ الدُّنْيَا حُلْوَةٌ خَضِرَةٌ وَإِنَّ اللَّهَ مُسْتَخْلِفُكُمْ فِيهَا فَيَنْظُرُ كَيْفَ تَعْمَلُونَ فَاتَّقُوا الدُّنْيَا وَاتَّقُوا النِّسَاءَ فَإِنَّ أَوَّلَ فِتْنَةِ بَنِي إِسْرَائِيلَ كَانَتْ فِي النِّسَاءِ»

"Indeed the Dunyaa is sweet and green. Allaah has made you to be vicegerents over it to see how you will behave. So fear the Dunyaa and beware of women. For indeed the first Fitnah that struck the Children of Israa'eel was related to the women."

He (ﷺ) also said:

«رُبَّ كَاسِيَةٍ فِي الدُّنْيَا عَارِيَةٍ فِي الْآخِرَةِ»

"Perhaps she who is clothed in the Dunyaa will be naked in the hereafter."

He (ﷺ) also said:

«صِنْفَانِ مِنْ أَهْلِ النَّارِ لَمْ أَرَهُمَا قَوْمٌ مَعَهُمْ سِيَاطٌ كَأَذْنَابِ الْبَقَرِ يَضْرِبُونَ بِهَا النَّاسَ وَنِسَاءٌ كَاسِيَاتٌ عَارِيَاتٌ مُمِيلَاتٌ مَائِلَاتٌ رُءُوسُهُنَّ كَأَسْنِمَةِ الْبُخْتِ الْمَائِلَةِ لَا يَدْخُلْنَ الْجَنَّةَ وَلَا يَجِدْنَ رِيحَهَا وَإِنَّ رِيحَهَا لَيُوجَدُ مِنْ مَسِيرَةِ كَذَا وَكَذَا»

"There are two classes from the people of the fire that I have yet to see : 1) A people who have whips that are similar to the tails of cows with which they beat the people. 2) Women who are clothed but naked; they sway when they walk and their heads will be high like a camel with humps. They will not enter Paradise nor will they smell its scent although its scent can be detected from a distance of such and such."

This is a severe warning against At-Tabarruj, uncovering, and wearing thin and short clothing; as well as swaying away from the truth and chastity and calling the people to lewdness and falsehood. It is also a severe warning against oppressing the people and transgressing against them; and it is a threat for the one who does this that he will be deprived of entering Paradise. We ask Allaah for safety from that.

From the greatest types of corruption is that many of the Muslim women imitate the disbelieving women from the Christians and their likes, in terms of wearing short clothing and displaying their hair and their beauty and styling their hair in the manner of the disbelievers and wicked people. They likewise attach extensions to their hair and wear artificial hair called wigs. The Prophet (ﷺ) said:

«مَنْ تَشَبَّهَ بِقَوْمٍ فَهُوَ مِنْهُمْ»

"Whoever imitates a people then he is from them."

That which this imitation and short clothing that makes the woman appear to be naked bring about, from corruption and Fitnah, as well as belittlement of the religion and scanty modesty, is known. Therefore, it is obligatory to sternly warn against this and to prevent the women from it, and be stern in doing so. This is because its end result is destructive and the corruption of it is great. It is not permissible to be lenient in this with the young girls. This is because their cultivation upon this would lead to them becoming accustomed to it and them despising

Indecency and Its Dangers | 23

anything that contradicts it once they become older. So, they will fall into this corruption, this prohibition, this feared Fitnah which the older women fall into.

Hence, have Taqwaa of Allaah and beware of that which Allaah has prohibited. Cooperate upon righteousness and piety and mutually invite one another to the truth and to be patient upon it. Know that Allaah, the Glorified, will ask you about that and He will recompense you for your actions; and He is with the patient, the pious, and the good-doers. So be patient and enjoin patience and have Taqwaa of Allaah and do good deeds; for indeed Allaah loves the good-doers.

There is no doubt that the obligation upon the leaders, from the rulers, judges, scholars, directors, and heads of the various committees, is greater that the obligation upon other than them and the danger upon them is greater. The Fitnah of them being silent is severe. It is not solely upon them to criticize (this action). Rather, the obligation is upon all of the Muslims; especially certain individuals; their seniors. More specifically, the guardians of the women and their husbands; they must repudiate this evil and the error that lies within it. They should be firm upon those who are lenient regarding this. Perhaps Allaah will remove from us that which has descended from calamities and guide us to the straight path.

It has been authentically reported from the Prophet (ﷺ) that he said:

«مَا مِنْ نَبِيٍّ بَعَثَهُ اللَّهُ فِي أُمَّةٍ قَبْلِي إِلَّا كَانَ لَهُ مِنْ أُمَّتِهِ حَوَارِيُّونَ وَأَصْحَابٌ يَأْخُذُونَ بِسُنَّتِهِ وَيَقْتَدُونَ بِأَمْرِهِ ثُمَّ إِنَّهَا

> تَخْلُفُ مِنْ بَعْدِهِمْ خُلُوفٌ يَقُولُونَ مَا لاَ يَفْعَلُونَ وَيَفْعَلُونَ مَا لاَ يُؤْمَرُونَ فَمَنْ جَاهَدَهُمْ بِيَدِهِ فَهُوَ مُؤْمِنٌ وَمَنْ جَاهَدَهُمْ بِلِسَانِهِ فَهُوَ مُؤْمِنٌ وَمَنْ جَاهَدَهُمْ بِقَلْبِهِ فَهُوَ مُؤْمِنٌ وَلَيْسَ وَرَاءَ ذَلِكَ مِنَ الإِيمَانِ حَبَّةُ خَرْدَلٍ»

"There was no Prophet Allaah sent before me to any Ummah except that he has disciples and companions who took to his Sunnah and followed his command. Then there succeeded them successors who said that which they did not do and did that which they were not commanded. So, he who struggles against them with his hand then he is a believer. He who struggles against them with his tongue then he is a believer. He who struggles against them with his heart then he is a believer, and there is not beyond that any fait even equivalent to a mustard seed."

I ask Allaah to give victory to his religion and to elevate his word and to rectify our leaders and to suppress falsehood by way of them and to give victory to the truth by way of them; likewise, to make upright his advisors and to give us, you, them, and the rest of the Muslims Tawfeeq in that which will rectify the people and the lands; in the worldly affairs and in the hereafter. Indeed, He is able to do all things and certain to respond. Sufficient for us is Allaah and He is the best Disposer of Affairs. There is no might nor power except with Allaah, the Most High, the Magnificent. May prayers, peace, and blessings be upon His slave and Messenger Muhammad, his family, and his companions and those who follow them until the Day of Recompense.

The Danger of Women Sharing the Work Arena of Men

All the praise is for Allaah, the Lord of all that exists. May prayers and peace be upon His trustworthy Messenger, his family, and companions, altogether. As to proceed:

Indeed, the call to the women entering the work arena of men, which leads to free-mixing—whether that be explicitly or hidden—with the argument that this is from that which the times necessitate and the present situation calls for it, is a very dangerous matter. It has dangerous implications and sour fruits and its end results are destructive. Not to mention that it opposes the legislative texts which command the woman to remain within her home and to establish the work which is specific to her within the homes.

He who wants to know that which free mixing brings about from corruption which cannot be enumerated, then let him look at those societies which have fallen into this severe trial—by their own volition or by force—objectively and sincerely (desiring) the truth, he will find (within those societies) destruction, on an individual level and on a societal level. (He will also find) determination to remove the woman from her home and protection of her family. We find that clearly written within many books; rather, within all of the various media outlets. This is only due to this destruction of the society and demolition of its structure.

The authentic and explicit evidence indicating the prohibition of seclusion with unrelated women and the prohibition of looking at them as well as the prohibition of the means which lead to falling into that which Allaah had prohibited, are very many; concluding the fact that free mixing leads to that which has a result that is blameworthy.

Removing the woman from her home, which is her kingdom and her primary domain, is removing her from that which her Fitrah and nature that Allaah created her with necessitates. Therefore, calling to the woman entering the work arena which is specifically for the men is an affair which is dangerous for the Islamic society, and from the greatest of its effects is free mixing which is considered to be from the greatest means to fornication, which destroys the society and is destructive to its value and morals.

It is known that Allaah has made the woman with a composition that it totally different from that of the man. He has made her to establish the work that which is within the home and to work amongst others similar to her (i.e., other women). This means that the involving the women in the work arena specific to the men is considered removing her from that which her composition and nature necessitates. This is a great crime against the woman and transgression against her. That in turn affects the generations of children, males and females. For they will miss out on cultivation, sensitivity, and affection. The one who fulfills this role—the mother—has neglected it and completely left off her domain, besides which it is not possible to find comfort and stability except within it. The current state of the societies in which this takes place is the most truthful witness for that which we say. Islaam has made for each of the two spouses certain obligations which are specific to them that they must fulfill in order that the societal structure will be complete within the home and outside of it.

The man must see after spending as well as earning a living while the woman takes care of the cultivation of the children, displaying affection, and tenderness as well as suckling, caretaking and the jobs which are appropriate for teaching the girls and running their schools as well as being doctors (for the females) and nurses for them and the likes, from the jobs which are specific to the women. The woman abandoning the obligations of the home is considered to be squandering the household along with whoever is within it. By way of this the destruction of the family is brought about, literally and figuratively, and with this the society becomes an entity which has no substance or import.

Allaah, the Majestic and High, says:

﴿ٱلرِّجَالُ قَوَّٰمُونَ عَلَى ٱلنِّسَآءِ بِمَا فَضَّلَ ٱللَّهُ بَعْضَهُمْ عَلَىٰ بَعْضٍ وَبِمَآ أَنفَقُوا۟ مِنْ أَمْوَٰلِهِمْ﴾

"Men are the protectors and maintainers of women, because Allaah has made one of them to excel the other, and because they spend (to support them) from their means." (An-Nisa 4:34)

The Sunnah of Allaah within His creation is that the authority is for the man over the woman and the man has a virtue over her, as the verse indicates. Allaah has commanded the woman to stay within her home and He has prohibited her from At-Tabarruj; this means that free mixing is prohibited for her; which is unrelated men and women intermingling within the same place, to work or buy and sell, or outings, or travel, etc. This is because the entrance of the woman into this field leads her to fall into the prohibited affairs and in this lied opposition to the command of Allaah and squandering of the rights of Allaah which are required legislatively for the Muslim female to establish.

The Book and the Sunnah have proven the prohibition of free mixing and the prohibition of all means which lead to it. Allaah, the Mighty and Majestic has stated:

﴿ وَقَرْنَ فِى بُيُوتِكُنَّ وَلَا تَبَرَّجْنَ تَبَرُّجَ ٱلْجَٰهِلِيَّةِ ٱلْأُولَىٰ وَأَقِمْنَ ٱلصَّلَوٰةَ وَءَاتِينَ ٱلزَّكَوٰةَ وَأَطِعْنَ ٱللَّهَ وَرَسُولَهُۥٓ إِنَّمَا يُرِيدُ ٱللَّهُ لِيُذْهِبَ عَنكُمُ ٱلرِّجْسَ أَهْلَ ٱلْبَيْتِ وَيُطَهِّرَكُمْ تَطْهِيرًا ۝ وَٱذْكُرْنَ مَا يُتْلَىٰ فِى بُيُوتِكُنَّ مِنْ ءَايَٰتِ ٱللَّهِ وَٱلْحِكْمَةِ إِنَّ ٱللَّهَ كَانَ لَطِيفًا خَبِيرًا ۝ ﴾

"And stay in your houses, and do not display yourselves like that of the times of ignorance, and perform As-Salât and give Zakat and obey Allaah and His Messenger. Allaah wishes only to remove Ar-Rijs (evil deeds and sins, etc.) from you, O members of the family (of the Prophet), and to purify you with a thorough purification. And remember (O you the members of the Prophet's family, the Graces of your Lord), that which is recited in your houses of the

Verses of Allaah and Al-Hikmah (i.e. Prophet's Sunnah) Verily, Allaah is Ever Most Courteous, Well-Acquainted with all things." (Al-Ahzab 33:33-34)

Allaah commanded the mothers of the believers—and all of the Muslim women and believing women enter into that—to remain within their homes due to that which it contains from safeguarding them and distancing them from the means to corruption. This is because going out without need will perhaps lead to At-Tabarruj just as it may lead to other evils.

He then commanded them to do righteous actions which will keep them away from lewdness and evil; this is by way of establishing the prayer, paying Zakat, and being obedient to Allaah and His Messenger (ﷺ). He then directed them to that which will bring benefit to them within the Dunyaa and the Hereafter; this is by having a constant connection with the Noble Qur'aan and the pure prophetic Sunnah which contain that which will rectify the hearts and purify them from the filth and impurities and will guide to the truth and that which is correct.

Allaah (سُبْحَانَهُ وَتَعَالَى) says:

﴿يَٰٓأَيُّهَا ٱلنَّبِىُّ قُل لِّأَزْوَٰجِكَ وَبَنَاتِكَ وَنِسَآءِ ٱلْمُؤْمِنِينَ يُدْنِينَ عَلَيْهِنَّ مِن جَلَٰبِيبِهِنَّ ۚ ذَٰلِكَ أَدْنَىٰٓ أَن يُعْرَفْنَ فَلَا يُؤْذَيْنَ ۗ وَكَانَ ٱللَّهُ غَفُورًا رَّحِيمًا ۝٥٩﴾

"O Prophet! Tell your wives and your daughters and the women of the believers to draw their cloaks (veils) all over their bodies (i.e., screen themselves completely except the eyes or one eye to see the way). That will be better, that they should be known (as free respectable women) so as not to be annoyed. And Allaah is Ever Oft-Forgiving, Most Merciful." (Al-Ahzab 33:59)

Allaah commanded his Prophet (ﷺ), who is the conveyor from his Lord, to tell his wives, daughters, and the believing women in general to draw their veils upon themselves; this includes the covering the entirety of their bodies with their cloak. This is when they desire to go out due to a need, in order that they should not be harmed by those who have sick hearts.

Since the affair is like this, what do you think regard her entering into the arena of the men and mixing with them and presenting her needs to them on the basis of employment and abandoning much of her femininity in order to be, by way of that, on par with them? She loses much of her modesty in order to attain a supposed equality between the sexes. Allaah, the Majestic and High, says:

﴿قُل لِّلْمُؤْمِنِينَ يَغُضُّوا۟ مِنْ أَبْصَٰرِهِمْ وَيَحْفَظُوا۟ فُرُوجَهُمْ ذَٰلِكَ أَزْكَىٰ لَهُمْ إِنَّ ٱللَّهَ خَبِيرٌۢ بِمَا يَصْنَعُونَ ۝ وَقُل لِّلْمُؤْمِنَٰتِ يَغْضُضْنَ مِنْ أَبْصَٰرِهِنَّ وَيَحْفَظْنَ فُرُوجَهُنَّ وَلَا يُبْدِينَ زِينَتَهُنَّ إِلَّا مَا ظَهَرَ مِنْهَا وَلْيَضْرِبْنَ بِخُمُرِهِنَّ عَلَىٰ جُيُوبِهِنَّ﴾

"Tell the believing men to lower their gaze (from looking at forbidden things), and protect their private parts (from illegal sexual acts, etc.). That is purer for them. Verily, Allaah is All-Aware of what they do. And tell the believing women to lower their gaze (from looking at forbidden things), and protect their private parts (from illegal sexual acts, etc.) and not to show off their adornment except only that which is apparent (like palms of hands or one eye or both eyes for necessity to see the way, or outer dress like veil, gloves, head-cover, apron, etc.), and to draw their veils all over their bodies." (An-Nur 24:30-31)

Allaah commands His Prophet (ﷺ) to convey to the believing men and women that they are to cling to lowering their gaze and safeguard their private parts from fornication. Then He clarified that this affair is purer for them. It is known that safeguarding the private parts from lewdness is only by avoiding its means, and without doubt, allowing the gaze to roam freely and free mixing between women and men in the workplace and other than it is from the greatest means for falling into lewdness. These are two affairs (lowering the gaze and safeguarding the private parts) which are (legislatively) desired from the believer are impossible to actualize whilst her works along with the unrelated woman as a coworker or partner in his occupation.

Without doubt, her entrance into this arena along with him or his entrance into the arena along with her is from the affairs which make it impossible to lower the gaze and safeguard one's private parts and thus attain purity and wholesomeness of the soul.

Likewise, Allaah commanded the believing women to lower their gaze and to safeguard their private parts and not to display their adornments with the exception of that which is apparent from it. Allaah commanded them to bring down their Khimaar over their bodies, which includes covering her head and face. This is because the Jayb is the place of the head and face. So how can one attain lowering of the gaze and safeguarding the private part and not displaying one's beauty when the woman has entered into the work arena of the men and they are free mixing with them in work; and free mixing is a means of falling into these evils. How can the Muslim woman attain lowering her gaze while she walks side by side with the unrelated man with the clam that she shares a job with him and is his equal in all that he does?

Islaam has prohibited all means which lead to prohibited matters. Due to this, Islaam has prohibited the women from sweetening their speech when speaking to men such that it would lead to lustfully desiring them; as He said:

﴿يَٰنِسَآءَ ٱلنَّبِىِّ لَسْتُنَّ كَأَحَدٍ مِّنَ ٱلنِّسَآءِ إِنِ ٱتَّقَيْتُنَّ فَلَا تَخْضَعْنَ بِٱلْقَوْلِ فَيَطْمَعَ ٱلَّذِى فِى قَلْبِهِۦ مَرَضٌ وَقُلْنَ قَوْلًا مَّعْرُوفًا ٣٢﴾

"O wives of the Prophet! You are not like any other women. If you keep your duty (to Allaah), then be not soft in speech, lest he in whose heart is a disease should be moved with desire, but speak in an honorable manner." (Al-Ahzab 33:32)

Meaning, a disease of lustful desire. So how is it possible to safeguard oneself from that when there is free mixing? From that which is clear is that if she enters the arena of men then it is inevitable that she will speak with them and they will speak to her. It is also inevitable that she will speak softly with them and they with her; and Shaytaan is behind that, beautifying and making it fair-seeming and calling to lewdness until they fall prey to him. Allaah is All-

Indecency and Its Dangers | 33

Wise and All-Knowing, thus He commanded the woman to wear the Hijaab. This is only because amongst the people there is the righteous and there is the wicked; the pure and the impure. Therefore, the Hijaab prevents—by the permission of Allaah—from Fitnah and it blocks its means. By way of it purity of the hearts is attained for the men and the women as well as distance from slanderous suspicions. Allaah said:

﴿وَإِذَا سَأَلْتُمُوهُنَّ مَتَاعًا فَسْـَٔلُوهُنَّ مِن وَرَآءِ حِجَابٍ ذَٰلِكُمْ أَطْهَرُ لِقُلُوبِكُمْ وَقُلُوبِهِنَّ﴾

"And when you ask (his wives) for anything you want, ask them from behind a screen, that is purer for your hearts and for their hearts." (Al-Ahzab 33:53)

The best Hijaab for the woman, after covering her face and her body with garments, is the Hijaab of the house. Islaam has prohibited her from mixing with strange men so that she should not subject herself to Fitnah directly or indirectly. It commands her to remain with her home and not to go out except due to a permissible need, whilst maintaining legislative etiquettes. Allaah has referred to the woman's remaining within the home as قرار This is from using lofty the meaning to refer to the affair; for within the home there lies stability for herself, comfort for her heart, and ease for her chest.

Her departure from this leads to uneasiness of the soul, worry within the heart, and tightness of the chest and it subjects her to things the end result of which is not praiseworthy.

Islaam has absolutely prohibited (a man) being secluded with the unrelated woman; this is to the exclusion of the relative. It has also prohibited her from traveling except with a Mahram, in order to block the means to corruption and close the door to sin and cut off the means of evil and a protection of the two parties (male and female) from the plots of Shaytaan. Due to this, it has been authentically narrated from the Prophet (ﷺ) that he said:

«مَا تَرَكْتُ بَعْدِي فِتْنَةً أَضَرَّ عَلَى الرِّجَالِ مِنَ النِّسَاءِ»

"I have not left behind a Fitnah more harmful for the men than the women."[1]

Some of the callers to free mixing cling to some of the apparent meanings of the legislative texts which are not understood and comprehended except by he whom Allaah has enlightened his heart and given Fiqh in the religion of Allaah, thus he brings the texts together and does not isolate them from one another. From that is the fact that some of the women went out with the Messenger (ﷺ) during some of the battles. The response to this is that their going out was along with their Mahrams for the purpose of beneficial affair does not bring about that which is feared, from corruption of their Eemaan and Taqwaa and the supervision of their Mahrams along with the observing of the Hijaab after the revelation of the verse, is in opposition to the state of many of the women of this time. It is known that the woman going out from her home to work differs completely from the state in which they went out with the Messenger (ﷺ) during the battles.

---

[1] Reported by Al-Bukhaaree and Muslim

Therefore, comparison between the two is considered comparing two things that are totally different. Also, how did the Salaf As-Saalih understand this? Without doubt, they were more knowledgeable regarding the meanings of the texts than other than them and they were closer to the practical application of the Book of Allaah and the Sunnah of His Messenger (ﷺ). Therefore, what was transmitted from them over the passing of time? Did they widen the sphere, as the callers to free mixing claim; so that there has come regarding this that the woman works within every realm from the realms of the men, crowding with them and mixing with them? Or did they understand that this was a specific issue which is not transitive to other situations?

If we research the Islamic conquests and battles over the passing of time we do not find this occurrence. As for that which is called to within this time from the woman entering into the battles as a soldier, carrying weapons and fighting like the man, no doubt it would lead to corruption and the loss of good character on the part of the armies; in the name of "entertaining the soldiers." This is because when the nature of the man connects with the nature of the woman—while being secluded—then there is between every man and woman from (natural) inclination, affability, and pleasure by way of speech and discourse, something which pulls one to the other. Closing the door to Fitnah is more prudent, safer and further from future regret.

Therefore, Islaam is very diligent upon bringing about benefit and repelling harm and closing the doors which lead to it. Free mixing between men and women within the workplace has a major effect in degradation of the Ummah and corruption of the society, as has preceded. This is because it is historically known, regarding ancient Roman and Greek civilizations and other than them, that the greatest means of their decline and collapse was the woman departing the domain that was specific to her and entering into the domain of the men and mixing with them. It is from that which leads to corruption of the manners of the men and their abandonment of that which drives their nation to purity, both literally and figuratively. The woman working outside of the home leads to the neglect on the part of the man and loss of the Ummah by way of breakdown of the family and its downfall as well as the corruption of the character of the children. It also leads to falling into that which opposes what Allaah has stated within His Book, from the authority of the man over the woman. Islaam is diligent in distancing the woman from all of that which opposes her natural make up. Therefore, it prohibits her from assuming general ruler-ship, such as presidency over the government and being a judge and every position which contains general responsibility. This is due to the statement of the Prophet (ﷺ)

«لَنْ يُفْلِحَ قَوْمٌ وَلَّوْا أَمْرَهُمْ امْرَأَةً»

"A people will never be successful who have a woman in charge of their affairs."[2]

Opening the door for her to enter into the work arena of the men is considered opposing that which Islaam desires;

---

[2] Reported by Al-Bukhaaree

from her happiness and stability. Therefore, Islaam has prohibited the woman being employed within other than her original position. It is affirmed by way of various experiences, specifically within the mixed societies, that the men and women are not equal in terms of natural disposition and in their make-up, not to mention that which has clearly come within the Book and the Sunnah regarding the difference in the natures and obligations. Those who call to the equality between the fair sex (the female) which is brought up wearing jewelry and in secluded dwellings, and the men, are ignorant or feigning ignorance of the foundational differences between the two.

We have mentioned from legislative evidence and actual occurrences that which proves the prohibition of free mixing and the woman participating within job field of the men; this (which we have mentioned) contains sufficiency and enough to convince the one who seeks the truth. However, seeing as how some people benefit from the speech of western and eastern men more than the benefit from the Speech of Allaah and His Messenger (ﷺ) and the speech of the Muslim scholars, then we see fit to transmit that which shows the recognition of western and eastern (non-Muslim) men of the harm of free mixing and its corruption; perhaps they will be convinced by this and know that what their magnificent religion came with, from the prohibition of free mixing is in fact nobility and protection of the women and safeguarding them from the means of harm and violation of their honor:

The English writer Lady Cooke said: "Indeed free mixing has an effect upon the men. Due to this the woman has experienced that which opposes her natural disposition. In proportion to the abundance of free mixing there is an abundance of illegitimate children. In this lies a great trial for the woman..." **She continued:** "Teach them to stay away from the men and inform them of the result of the hidden plot against them."

Schopenhauer, the German, said: "Say it is a great lapse in the gradual decline of our condition for the woman to share with the man in his lofty position and his high rank. It is easy for her to be conquered and vilely exploited until the society is corrupted by way of her gaining authority and implementation of her views."

Lord Byron said: "If you were to reflect, O reader, upon the state of the woman during the time of the ancient Greeks you will find that she was in an unauthentic state which opposed her natural makeup. You will see, just as I do, the obligation of the women being preoccupied with household duties whilst fulfilling them with excellence and observance of a good manner of dress therein. It is necessary that she be shielded from mixing with others (men)."

The British man, Samuel Smills, said: "The organization which calls for the woman to be occupied with work, no matter what emanates from it from refinement of the land, the end result of it is the destruction of the home life. This is because it is destruction of the fabric of the home and the pillars of the family and the connection to the society will be torn; the wife will be detached from the husband, and the children will be lost from the relatives, the affair will come to be a type of matter which has no end result except that the character of the woman will be debased. Indeed, the true job of the woman is to establish the obligations (of the home); such as the cultivation of the household, cultivating the children and seeing after the means to her livelihood. This, in addition to taking care of the needs of her household. However, working (outside the home) will strip her away from all these obligations to the point that the home will come to be such that it is not a home. The children will come to be a product of a lack of proper upbringing and will bear the signs of neglect. Spousal love will dissipate and the woman will no longer be the amiable wife and a loving companion for the man. She will come to be his colleague in work and toil. This will bring about affects that which erase most ideological and character humility upon which virtue is based."

Doctor Eda Elain said: "The reason for the decline of the family structure in America and the subtle cause for many of the crimes within the society is that the wife has abandoned her home in order to double (income) within the family. There has been an increase in this and the morals have declined..." She went on to say: "Experience has affirmed that the return of the woman into the sanctuary (her home) is the sole path to the salvation of the new generation from the destructive path which it is traversing upon."

One of the members of the American congress said: "Indeed the woman can better serve the government by remaining within the home which is the foundation of the family unit."

Another member said: "Indeed when God distinguished the woman with the ability to bear children, he did not demand for her to abandon them in order to work outside the home. Rather, He made it such that her primary concern should be remaining within the home in order to see after these children."

Schopenhauer, the German, also said: "Leave the woman to be absolutely and completely free, without any watcher over her, then meet me after a year, and you will see the result; do not forget that we are all responsible for having virtue, chastity, and good manners. If I die, then say: he was wrong, or he was right, being truthful in that."

Doctor Mustapha Hosni As-Sibaa'ee (رحمه الله), mentioned all these quotes within his book: The Woman, between Islamic Jurisprudence and the Constitution. Had we willed to mention at length that which the intellectuals of the west have stated regarding the harm of free mixing, which is the end result of the woman entering into the work arena of the men, then the speech would be lengthy. However, this useful indication is sufficient, thus there is no need for lengthy speech.

In summary, the woman remaining within her home and establishing that which is obligatory upon her is from managing it—after the establishment of her religious obligations—is the affair which is appropriate for her nature and her disposition and being. It contains her rectification and the rectification of the society as well as the upcoming generation. If she has spare time then she can be allowed to enter into the arenas of the women; such as teaching women as well as medical services and nursing them and the likes, from that which is within the work sphere of the women, as has preceded. In her (true) occupation there lies that which will occupy her, as well as cooperation with the men in the functions of the society and the means of its development, each in their own respective capacity. We do not forget here the roles of the mothers of the believers—may Allaah be pleased with them and those who traversed upon their path—and that which they established from teaching the Ummah, directing, guiding, and conveying from Allaah and His Messenger (); so may Allaah reward them for that with good, and increase the Muslims today with their likes, along with proper covering and safeguarding (themselves) and farness away from free mixing with the men in their workplace. We ask Allaah to enlighten everyone with that which is obligatory upon them and to assist them in performing it in the manner which is pleasing to Him; and to protect everyone from the means of Fitnah and the acts of corruption and the plots of Shaytaan. Indeed He is Generous and Kind. May prayers and peace be upon His slave and Messenger; our Prophet Muhammad, his family and companions.

✿ ✿ ✿

The Ruling Regarding Intermingling While Studying

All of the Praise is for Allaah. May prayers and peace be upon the Messenger of Allaah to proceed:

I have reviewed that which was circulated within the newspaper entitled As-Siyaasah, which was published on the 24th of Rajab in the year 1404, H. Issue no. 5644, which was ascribed to the Head of the University of Sanaa'. The Dr. Abdul-Azeez Al-Maqaalih, who claims then that the call for the female students to be separate from the males is something which opposes the legislation. He used as evidence for the permissibility of free-mixing that the Muslims during the time of the Messenger (ﷺ) used to perform the prayer within one Masjid, the men and the women. And he said: **"Due to this, it is a must that their study be within one and the same place."**

I deem this speech from this Dean of an Islamic University within an Islamic land to be strange. One who is required to direct those under his care, from the men and the women, to that which contains happiness and success in the Dunyaa as well as the hereafter. And indeed, we belong to Allaah and to Him we shall return and there is neither might nor power except with Allaah.

Without doubt this speech contains a great crime against the legislation of Islam. This is because the legislation does not call to free-mixing, such that the call to its prevention is in opposition to the legislation. Rather, Islam prevents it sternly as Allaah, the Mighty and Majestic, said:

﴿ وَقَرْنَ فِي بُيُوتِكُنَّ وَلَا تَبَرَّجْنَ تَبَرُّجَ ٱلْجَٰهِلِيَّةِ ٱلْأُولَىٰ ﴾

"And stay in your houses, and do not display yourselves like that of the times of ignorance." (Al-Ahzab 33:33)

And, likewise, Allaah, also said:

﴿ يَٰٓأَيُّهَا ٱلنَّبِيُّ قُل لِّأَزْوَٰجِكَ وَبَنَاتِكَ وَنِسَآءِ ٱلْمُؤْمِنِينَ يُدْنِينَ عَلَيْهِنَّ مِن جَلَٰبِيبِهِنَّ ذَٰلِكَ أَدْنَىٰٓ أَن يُعْرَفْنَ فَلَا يُؤْذَيْنَ وَكَانَ ٱللَّهُ غَفُورًا رَّحِيمًا ۝ ﴾

"O Prophet! Tell your wives and your daughters and the women of the believers to draw their cloaks (veils) all over their bodies (i.e., screen themselves completely except the eyes or one eye to see the way). That will be better, that they should be known (as free respectable women) so as not to be annoyed. And Allaah is Ever Oft-Forgiving, Most Merciful." (Al-Ahzab 33:59)

Allaah also (سُبْحَانَهُ وَتَعَالَى) said:

﴿ وَقُل لِّلْمُؤْمِنَٰتِ يَغْضُضْنَ مِنْ أَبْصَٰرِهِنَّ وَيَحْفَظْنَ فُرُوجَهُنَّ وَلَا يُبْدِينَ زِينَتَهُنَّ إِلَّا مَا ظَهَرَ مِنْهَا وَلْيَضْرِبْنَ بِخُمُرِهِنَّ عَلَىٰ جُيُوبِهِنَّ وَلَا يُبْدِينَ زِينَتَهُنَّ إِلَّا لِبُعُولَتِهِنَّ أَوْ ءَابَآئِهِنَّ أَوْ ءَابَآءِ بُعُولَتِهِنَّ أَوْ أَبْنَآئِهِنَّ أَوْ أَبْنَآءِ بُعُولَتِهِنَّ أَوْ إِخْوَٰنِهِنَّ أَوْ بَنِىٓ إِخْوَٰنِهِنَّ أَوْ بَنِىٓ أَخَوَٰتِهِنَّ أَوْ نِسَآئِهِنَّ أَوْ مَا مَلَكَتْ أَيْمَٰنُهُنَّ أَوِ ٱلتَّٰبِعِينَ غَيْرِ أُو۟لِى ٱلْإِرْبَةِ مِنَ ٱلرِّجَالِ أَوِ ٱلطِّفْلِ ٱلَّذِينَ لَمْ يَظْهَرُوا۟ عَلَىٰ عَوْرَٰتِ

$$\text{ٱلنِّسَآءِۖ وَلَا يَضْرِبْنَ بِأَرْجُلِهِنَّ لِيُعْلَمَ مَا يُخْفِينَ مِن زِينَتِهِنَّۚ وَتُوبُوٓا۟ إِلَى ٱللَّهِ جَمِيعًا أَيُّهَ ٱلْمُؤْمِنُونَ لَعَلَّكُمْ تُفْلِحُونَ ۝}$$

"And tell the believing women to lower their gaze (from looking at forbidden things), and protect their private parts (from illegal sexual acts, etc.) and not to show off their adornment except only that which is apparent (like palms of hands or one eye or both eyes for necessity to see the way, or outer dress like veil, gloves, head-cover, apron, etc.), and to draw their veils all over Juyubihinna (i.e. their bodies, faces, necks and bosoms, etc.) and not to reveal their adornment except to their husbands, their fathers, their husband's fathers, their sons, their husband's sons, their brothers or their brother's sons, or their sister's sons, or their (Muslim) women (i.e. their sisters in Islâm), or the (female) slaves whom their right hands possess, or old male servants who lack vigour, or small children who have no sense of the shame of sex. And let them not stamp their feet so as to reveal what they hide of their adornment. And all of you beg Allâh to forgive you all, O believers, that you may be successful." (An-Nur 24:31)

And Allaah (سُبْحَانَهُ وَتَعَالَى) said:

$$\text{﴿ يَٰٓأَيُّهَا ٱلَّذِينَ ءَامَنُوا۟ لَا تَدْخُلُوا۟ بُيُوتَ ٱلنَّبِيِّ إِلَّآ أَن يُؤْذَنَ لَكُمْ إِلَىٰ طَعَامٍ غَيْرَ نَٰظِرِينَ إِنَىٰهُ وَلَٰكِنْ إِذَا دُعِيتُمْ فَٱدْخُلُوا۟ فَإِذَا طَعِمْتُمْ فَٱنتَشِرُوا۟ وَلَا مُسْتَـْٔنِسِينَ لِحَدِيثٍۚ إِنَّ ذَٰلِكُمْ كَانَ يُؤْذِى ٱلنَّبِيَّ فَيَسْتَحْىِۦ مِنكُمْۖ وَٱللَّهُ لَا يَسْتَحْىِۦ مِنَ ٱلْحَقِّۚ وَإِذَا سَأَلْتُمُوهُنَّ مَتَٰعًا}$$

$$\text{فَسْـَٔلُوهُنَّ مِن وَرَآءِ حِجَابٍ ذَٰلِكُمْ أَطْهَرُ لِقُلُوبِكُمْ وَقُلُوبِهِنَّ وَمَا كَانَ لَكُمْ أَن تُؤْذُوا۟ رَسُولَ ٱللَّهِ وَلَآ أَن تَنكِحُوٓا۟ أَزْوَٰجَهُۥ مِنۢ بَعْدِهِۦٓ أَبَدًا إِنَّ ذَٰلِكُمْ كَانَ عِندَ ٱللَّهِ عَظِيمًا ۝}$$

"O you who believe! Enter not the Prophet's houses, except when leave is given to you for a meal, (and then) not (so early as) to wait for its preparation. But when you are invited, enter, and when you have taken your meal, disperse, without sitting for a talk. Verily, such (behavior) annoys the Prophet, and he is shy of (asking) you (to go), but Allaah is not shy of (telling you) the truth. And when you ask (his wives) for anything you want, ask them from behind a screen, that is purer for your hearts and for their hearts. And it is not (right) for you that you should annoy Allâh's Messenger, nor that you should ever marry his wives after him (his death). Verily! With Allâh that shall be an enormity." (Al-Ahzab 33:53)

Within these noble verses lies a clear indication for legislation of the women remaining within their homes as a precaution from Fitnah; unless there is a need which calls for her to go out; moreover, Allaah warned her against At-Tabarruj (displaying her beauty) in the manner of the days of pre-Islamic ignorance; and this is to display her adornments and body parts amongst men.

It has been authentically narrated from the Messenger of Allaah (ﷺ) that he said:

$$\text{«مَا تَرَكْتُ بَعْدِي فِتْنَةً أَضَرَّ عَلَى الرِّجَالِ مِنَ النِّسَاءِ»}$$

> "I have not left behind me a Fitnah more harmful upon the men than the women."

This Hadeeth is agreed upon by Al-Bukhaaree and Muslim from the Hadeeth of Usaamah ibn Zayd (رَضِيَ ٱللَّهُ عَنْهُ). Muslim reported with his Saheeh on the authority of Usaamah as well as Sa'eed bin Zayd ibn Amr ibn Nufayl (رَضِيَ ٱللَّهُ عَنْهُمْ).

Likewise, there has come in the Saheeh on the authority of Abu Sa'eed al-Khudree may Allaah be pleased with him that the Prophet (صَلَّى ٱللَّهُ عَلَيْهِ وَسَلَّمَ) said:

«إِنَّ الدُّنْيَا حُلْوَةٌ خَضِرَةٌ وَإِنَّ اللَّهَ مُسْتَخْلِفُكُمْ فِيهَا فَيَنْظُرُ كَيْفَ تَعْمَلُونَ فَاتَّقُوا الدُّنْيَا وَاتَّقُوا النِّسَاءَ فَإِنَّ أَوَّلَ فِتْنَةِ بَنِي إِسْرَائِيلَ كَانَتْ فِي النِّسَاءِ»

> "Indeed, the Dunyaa is sweet and green. Allaah has made you to be vicegerents over it to see how you will behave. So, fear the Dunyaa and beware of women. For indeed the first Fitnah that struck the Children of Israa'eel was related to the women."

Indeed, the Messenger of Allaah (صَلَّى ٱللَّهُ عَلَيْهِ وَسَلَّمَ) has spoken the truth for indeed the Fitnah regarding them is great especially within this time when most of them have removed the Hijaab and they display their adornments with At-Tabarruj of the pre-Islamic days of ignorance and by way of it much lewdness and the evil is brought about and there is much reluctance from the youth and the young ladies regarding the legislation of Allaah from marriage within many of the lands. Allaah, the Glorified, has clarified that the Hijaab is more pure for the hearts of everyone. This indicates that removing it is nearer to filth for the hearts of everyone and the deviation from the path of truth. It is known that the female student sitting along with the male student for the purpose of study is from greatest means to Fitnah. And it is from the means of abandonment of Hijaab which Allaah has legislated for the believing women and He has prohibited them from displaying their adornments to others whom Allaah has clarified within the aforementioned verse within Surah An-Nur. He who claims that the affair of the Hijaab is specific for the mothers of the believers, then he has made a farfetched claim and he has opposed many text which indicate the generality of the ruling. And he has opposed as well the statement of Allaah:

﴿ذَٰلِكُمْ أَطْهَرُ لِقُلُوبِكُمْ وَقُلُوبِهِنَّ﴾

"That is purer for your hearts and for their hearts."
(Al-Ahzab 33:53)

Therefore, it is not permissible for it to be said that the Hijaab is pure for the hearts of the mothers of the believers and the men of the companions, may Allaah be pleased with them, to the exclusion of those who came after them. And there is no doubt that the those who came after them are more in need of Hijaab than the mothers of the believers and the men from amongst the companions due to that which there is between them from great differences as it relates to the strength of Eemaan and their enlightenment upon the truth. For indeed, the companions, may Allaah be pleased with them, were men and women. And from amongst them were the mothers of the believers and they are the best of the people after the Prophets and the most virtuous of generations by way of the textual evidence mentioned by the Messenger

(ﷺ) mentioned in the two Saheehs. Therefore, if the Hijaab were pure for their hearts, then those who came after them are more in need of this purity and more in need of it than those who came before them. This is also due to the fact that with regards to the text that have come within the Book and the Sunnah it is not permissible to specify them for anyone from the Ummah unless there is authentic evidence indicating the specification. Therefore, it is general for the entirety of the Ummah, whether within his time (ﷺ) or after it up until the day of judgement. This is because Allaah, the Glorified, sent His Messenger (ﷺ) to the two classes (mankind and the jinn) within his time (ﷺ) as well as those who came after up until the day of judgement as Allaah, the Mighty and Majestic, mentioned:

﴿قُلْ يَٰٓأَيُّهَا ٱلنَّاسُ إِنِّى رَسُولُ ٱللَّهِ إِلَيْكُمْ جَمِيعًا﴾

"Say (O Muhammad ﷺ): "O mankind! Verily, I am sent to you all as the Messenger of Allaah." (Al-A'raf 7:158)

Likewise, Allaah, the Exalted, said:

﴿وَمَآ أَرْسَلْنَٰكَ إِلَّا كَآفَّةً لِّلنَّاسِ بَشِيرًا وَنَذِيرًا وَلَٰكِنَّ أَكْثَرَ ٱلنَّاسِ لَا يَعْلَمُونَ ۝﴾

"And We have not sent you (O Muhammad ﷺ) except as a giver of glad tidings and a warner to all mankind, but most of men know not." (Saba' 34:28)

Thus, the Noble Qur'aan was not revealed for the people of the era of the Prophet (ﷺ) rather it was revealed to them as well as those who came after them from whoever the Book of Allaah should reach as Allaah, the Exalted, said:

﴿هَٰذَا بَلَٰغٌ لِّلنَّاسِ وَلِيُنذَرُوا۟ بِهِۦ وَلِيَعْلَمُوٓا۟ أَنَّمَا هُوَ إِلَٰهٌ وَٰحِدٌ وَلِيَذَّكَّرَ أُو۟لُوا۟ ٱلْأَلْبَٰبِ ۝﴾

"This (Qur'ân) is a Message for mankind (and a clear proof against them), in order that they may be warned thereby, and that they may know that He is the only One Ilâh (God - Allâh) - (none has the right to be worshipped but Allâh), and that men of understanding may take heed." (Ibrahim 14:52)

And likewise, Allaah (سُبْحَانَهُ وَتَعَالَى) said:

﴿وَأُوحِىَ إِلَىَّ هَٰذَا ٱلْقُرْءَانُ لِأُنذِرَكُم بِهِۦ وَمَنۢ بَلَغَ﴾

"This Qur'aan has been revealed to me that I may therewith warn you and whomsoever it may reach." (Al-An'am 6:19)

The women during the era of the Prophet (ﷺ) did not used to free mix with the men—neither within the Masaajid nor the marketplaces—with the type of free-mixing which the callers to rectification, prohibit today and the Qur'aan and Sunnah as scholars of the Ummah warn against its Fitnah. Rather, the women within the Masaajid used to pray behind the men in the last rows distant from them. The Prophet (ﷺ) used to say:

«خَيْرُ صُفُوفِ الرِّجَالِ أَوَّلُهَا وَشَرُّهَا آخِرُهَا وَخَيْرُ صُفُوفِ النِّسَاءِ آخِرُهَا وشرها أولها»

"The best rows for the men are the first rows and the worst of them are the last of them. The best rows for the women are the last rows and the worst are the first of them."[3]

This was done as a means of precaution from Fitnah. The last rows of the men would be near to the first rows of the women. The men during the time of the Prophet (ﷺ) were commanded to delay turning away from the prayer until the women had departed and left the Masjid in order that the men would not mix with them at the doors of the Masaajid. This is in spite of that which they were upon from Eemaan and Taqwaa. So how about the state of those who come after them?

The women used to be prohibited from walking in the middle of the path and they were commanded to take to the outer edges of the pathway as a precaution from crowding with the men and Fitnah by way of some of them touching one another as they passed to the pathway.

Allaah, the Glorified, commanded the women of the believers to draw their outer-garments upon their bodies in order that their beauty may be concealed as a means of precaution from being put to trial by way of them. And He has prohibited them from displaying their beauty to other than those who Allaah has named within His Mighty Book as a means to block the pathway to Fitnah and an encouragement to take to the means of chastity and farness way from that which will cause corruption and free-mixing. So how can it be permissible for the Headmaster of the University of Sanaa', may Allaah guide him and make him upright, after all of this called to free-mixing and claim

---

[3] Reported by Muslim

that Islam calls to it and that the college is similar to the Masjid and that the study times are similar to the times of Salah. It is known that the difference is great and contrast between the two is clear for the one who has intellect regarding Allaah, His commands, and His prohibitions and who Allaah has given knowledge of the wisdom in His legislation to His servants and that which Allaah has clarified within His Magnificent Book from rulings as it relates to men and women. How can it be permissible for the believer to say that the female student sitting along with the male student for the purpose of study is similar to her sitting amongst her sisters within their ranks behind the men? No one would say this that has the least amount of Eemaan and insight and understands the reality of that which he says. This is the case even if there were the presence of the legislated Hijaab so how about if she were to sit along with the male student for the purpose of study while engaging in At-Tabarruj and displaying her beauty along with looks that cause Fitnah and speech which pulls to Fitnah. And Allaah's aid is sought. And there is neither might nor power except with Allaah.

Allaah, the Majestic, has stated:

﴿ أَفَلَمْ يَسِيرُوا۟ فِى ٱلْأَرْضِ فَتَكُونَ لَهُمْ قُلُوبٌ يَعْقِلُونَ بِهَآ أَوْ ءَاذَانٌ يَسْمَعُونَ بِهَا ۖ فَإِنَّهَا لَا تَعْمَى ٱلْأَبْصَـٰرُ وَلَـٰكِن تَعْمَى ٱلْقُلُوبُ ٱلَّتِى فِى ٱلصُّدُورِ ﴾

"Verily, it is not the eyes that grow blind, but it is the hearts which are in the breasts that grow blind." (Al-Hajj 22:46)

As for the statement of the Headmaster: **"The reality is that Muslims during the era of the Messenger (ﷺ) used to perform prayer within the same Masjid; the men along with the women. Due to this, it is a must that their study be in one and the same place,"** The response regarding this is that it is said this is correct; however, the women were at the back of the Masjid along with observance of proper Hijaab and careful consideration to preserve themselves from that which would cause Fitnah and the men were at the foremost part of the Masjid. So, they would listen to the admonition and the sermons and participate within the prayer and learn the rulings of the religion from that which they heard and saw. The Prophet (ﷺ) on the day of 'Eid would go to the women after he had admonished the men and he would admonish them and he would remind them due to the fact that they were far away from where they would be able to hear his sermon. All of this is clear.

The problem only comes in as it relates to the statement of the Headmaster of the University of Sanaa', may Allaah guide him and rectify his heart and give him understanding of the religion. He said: **"...due to this it is a must that study be in one and the same place,"** How can it be conceivable to liken study within our time to the prayer of the men within the Masjid along with the fact that the differences between the two are well known? Due to this, those who call to rectification call to the women being clearly distinct from the men in the affairs of study. And that there be a barrier between the two and that the boys should be on one level and the girls on another in order that they may learn from the teachers at ease without wearing Hijaab and without difficulty. This is because the timeframe for teaching is long as opposed to the timeframe for the prayer. Also, learning the various sciences from the teachers within a specific place is better for all parties involved and further for them from the means of Fitnah and safer for the youth. Also, because having the youth to be separated in the schools away from the young ladies is safer for them from Fitnah. However, it is also nearer to giving due consideration to their studies and busying themselves with them as well as excellence in terms of listening to the teachers and taking the various sciences from them while being far away from looking at the girls and being preoccupied by way of them and exchanging poisonous looks and speech which calls to wickedness. As for his claim, may Allaah rectify him, that the call to the female students being removed from studying in a mixed (setting) opposes the legislation then this is a claim that has no basis. Rather, this (separating the two genders) indeed is from sincerity for Allaah to his servants and it is a means of safeguarding ones religion and to act in accordance with that which has proceeded from the Qur'anic verses and the noble Prophetic Hadeeths.

My advice to the Headmaster of the University of Sana'a is that he has Taqwaa of Allaah, the Mighty and Majestic. That he repents to Him, Glorified and Exalted be He, from that which has emanated from him and that he return to that which is correct and that he return to the truth. For indeed, returning to that is a virtue and it is an evidence that he desires to direct the students of knowledge to the truth and right conduct. And Allaah, the Glorified, is asked that He guide us all to the path of uprightness and that He give us refuge from speaking regarding Him without knowledge and from going astray and from the whispers of Shaytaan. I also ask Him, Glorified be He, to give the scholars of the Muslims and their leaders success in every place towards that which will rectify the lands and the servants with their lives and their hereafter and that He guide us all to His straight path. Indeed, He is Kind and Generous. May prayers and peace be upon our Prophet Muhammad, his family, his companions, and those who follow them in excellence until the day of recompense.

The Danger of Women Teaching Boys at the Primary School Level

I have reviewed that which was published within the city paper issue no. 3898 dated 30th of Safar year 1396 H.; written by she who calls her self Noorah bint 'Abdullah with the title Face to Face. The summary of the article is that the aforementioned Noorah attended a meeting along with some of the women in the presence of the Dean of Education in Jeddah whose name was Faa'izah. Noorah ascribed to Faa'izah that she deemed it to be strange that there were no female teachers teaching our male children at the primary school level, even if up to the 5th grade. The aforementioned, Noorah, used as evidence means which were inappropriate within her article. Although, I thank Faa'izah and Noorah as well as their colleagues for their concern with the subject of teaching our male children and their diligence upon benefiting them, I deem it is an obligation to draw attention to that which the suggestion contains from harm and evil results. And, the fact that placing the women in charge of teaching the boys at the primary level will lead to their free-mixing with adolescents and those who are of the age of puberty from the male children. This is because some of the boys do not attend primary school until they are of adolescent age. Some of them are perhaps in puberty. This is because when the boy reaches ten years of age he is considered to an adolescent and, his nature causes him to incline towards females. This is because those similar to him in age could quite possibly marry and do that which the men do.

There is another affair and it is the fact that the women teaching the boys at the introductory level will lead to free-mixing, then this will extend up until the other grades; so therefore, it is an opening of the door of free-mixing at all levels without doubt. It is known that which free-mixing for the purpose of education brings about from great evils and the disgusting results which have occurred with those who utilize this type of teaching method within the other lands. Anyone who has the slightest amount of knowledge regarding the legislative evidences and their reality of the Ummah within this time from those who have Islamic insight regarding our sons and daughters will know this beyond a shadow of a doubt and they will believe that this suggestion came from Shaytaan or his deputies speaking upon the tongue of Faa'izah and Noorah. Without doubt it is from that which would please our enemies; the enemies of Islam, and it is that which they call to, secretly and openly. Due to this, I see that it is obligatory to close this door with the utmost wisdom and that our male children should remain being taught by men at each level, just as our daughters should be taught by female teachers at each level. By way of this, we will safeguard our religion and our daughters and remain superior to our enemies. We expect from our respected female teachers that they should exert effort with all sincerity, truthfulness, and patience in teaching our girls. And, our men should establish with all sincerity, truthfulness, and patience the teaching of our boys at each level.

From that which is known is that the men are more patient regarding teaching the boys and firmer as it relates to them and more authoritative over them than the female teachers at each level. It is likewise known that the boys at the primary school level and above have a level of fear and respect for the male teacher and they listen to that which he says more so and in a more complete manner than that which would take place if the one who were to teach them was from the women. This is in addition to that which this contains from the cultivation of the boys at this level to have the characteristics of men and to have their forbearance, their patience, and their strength. It has been reported from the Prophet (ﷺ) that he said:

»مُرُوا أَوْلَادَكُمْ بِالصَّلَاةِ وَهُمْ أَبْنَاءُ سَبْعِ سِنِينَ وَاضْرِبُوهُمْ عَلَيْهَا وَهُمْ أَبْنَاءُ عَشْرِ سِنِينَ وَفَرِّقُوا بَيْنَهُمْ فِي الْمَضَاجِعِ«

"Teach the children to pray when they are seven and physically discipline them regarding it at ten years of age and separate them in their sleeping arrangements."[4]

This Hadeeth indicates that which we have mentioned from the danger of free-mixing between the boys and the girls within one place.

The evidences for this from the Book and the Sunnah, as well as the current affairs of the Ummah are many. We will not mention them here due to the desire to keep this statement summarized. And, in the knowledge of our government, May Allaah grant it success, and the knowledge of the Minster of Education, as well as the knowledge of the President of Girls Education, and their

---

[4] Reported by Ahmad and Aboo Dawood and al-Hakim, as well as As-Suyootee, who all attested to its authenticity.

wisdom, (may Allaah grant all of them success) there lies sufficiency from having to go at length regarding this subject.

I ask Allaah to grant us all success in that which contains rectification for the Ummah and its safety and uprightness as well as the uprightness of our youth, males and females, and there happiness in the Dunyaa as well as the hereafter. Indeed, He is the All-Hearing and He is All-Near. May prayers and peace be upon our Prophet Muhammad, his family and his companions.

Evil Affairs Which Must Be Avoided

All the praise is for Allaah, the Lord of all that exists. I send prayers and peace upon the best of His creation, our Prophet Muhammad, his family, and his companions, and those who follow his Sunnah and his guidance up until the day of recompense.

As to proceed:

Indeed, the greatest of the favors which Allaah has bestowed upon His servants is the favor of Al-Islam and guidance by way of following the legislation of the best of creation. And this is due to that which it contains from goodness and happiness in the Dunyaa as well as success, safety, and security on the day of judgement for the one who clings to it and traverses upon this methodology. It is not hidden that Islam has come with the preservation of the nobility of the women and safeguarding her and giving her a status that is befitting of her. And it has encouraged her to stay far away from that which will sully or remove her nobility. Due to this, it has been prohibited for her to be secluded with unrelated men. And, she has been prohibited from travelling without a mahram. She likewise has been prohibited from At-Tabarruj which Allaah has criticized as being indicative of the pre-Islamic days of ignorance due to it being from the means which lead to Fitnah and the appearance of lewdness.

Allaah, the Might and Majestic, said:

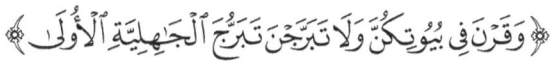

"And stay in your houses, and do not display yourselves like that of the times of ignorance." (Al-Ahzab 33:33)

At-Tabarruj is to display one's beauty and those affairs which will put one to trial. Allaah has prohibited her from free-mixing with men who are unrelated to her and He has prohibited her as well from sweetness in her speech when speaking to men, due to this being from the means of Fitnah and the desire for lewd acts; as Allaah the Mighty and Majestic has said:

$$\textit{﴿يَٰنِسَآءَ ٱلنَّبِيِّ لَسۡتُنَّ كَأَحَدٖ مِّنَ ٱلنِّسَآءِ إِنِ ٱتَّقَيۡتُنَّ فَلَا تَخۡضَعۡنَ بِٱلۡقَوۡلِ فَيَطۡمَعَ ٱلَّذِي فِي قَلۡبِهِۦ مَرَضٞ وَقُلۡنَ قَوۡلٗا مَّعۡرُوفٗا ۝﴾}$$

"O wives of the Prophet! You are not like any other women. If you keep your duty (to Allaah), then be not soft in speech, lest he in whose heart is a disease should be moved with desire, but speak in an honorable manner." (Al-Ahzab 33:32)

The sickness here refers to the sickness of desire. Allaah has likewise has commanded her to have modesty in her dress and He has obligated the Hijaab upon her due to that which it contains from protection for her and purity of the hearts of all parties.

Allaah, the Exalted, has said:

$$\textit{﴿يَٰٓأَيُّهَا ٱلنَّبِيُّ قُل لِّأَزۡوَٰجِكَ وَبَنَاتِكَ وَنِسَآءِ ٱلۡمُؤۡمِنِينَ يُدۡنِينَ عَلَيۡهِنَّ مِن جَلَٰبِيبِهِنَّۚ ذَٰلِكَ أَدۡنَىٰٓ أَن يُعۡرَفۡنَ فَلَا يُؤۡذَيۡنَۗ وَكَانَ ٱللَّهُ غَفُورٗا رَّحِيمٗا ۝﴾}$$

"O Prophet! Tell your wives and your daughters and the women of the believers to draw their cloaks (veils) all over their bodies (i.e., screen themselves completely except the eyes or one eye to see the way). That will be better, that they should be known (as free respectable women) so as not to be annoyed. And Allaah is Ever Oft-Forgiving, Most Merciful." (Al-Ahzab 33:59)

Likewise, Allaah, the Exalted, has said:

﴿ وَإِذَا سَأَلْتُمُوهُنَّ مَتَٰعًا فَسْـَٔلُوهُنَّ مِن وَرَآءِ حِجَابٍۚ ذَٰلِكُمْ أَطْهَرُ لِقُلُوبِكُمْ وَقُلُوبِهِنَّ ﴾

"And when you ask (his wives) for anything you want, ask them from behind a screen, that is purer for your hearts and for their hearts." (Al-Ahzab 33:53)

The female companions (رضي الله عنهن), adhered to the command of Allaah and His Messenger (صلى الله عليه وسلم). And thus they hastened to wear the Hijaab and to cover themselves from foreign men. Aboo Dawood has reported within authentic chain of narration from Umm Salamah (رضي الله عنها), as she said: "When this verses was revealed, the women of the Ansar went out as if they were crows upon their heads from the clothing that was upon them and they were covered in black garments which they wore…"

Imam Ahmad as well Aboo Dawood and Ibn Majah reported on the authority of the mother of the believers, 'Aisha (رضي الله عنها), that she said:

> «كَانَ الرُّكْبَانُ يَمُرُّونَ بِنَا وَنَحْنُ مَعَ رَسُولِ اللَّهِ صلى الله عليه وسلم مُحْرِمَاتٌ فَإِذَا حَاذَوْا بِنَا سَدَلَتْ إِحْدَانَا جِلْبَابَهَا مِنْ رَأْسِهَا إِلَى وَجْهِهَا فَإِذَا جَاوَزُونَا كَشَفْنَاهُ»

"The riders used to pass by us while we were in the state of Ihram along with the Messenger of Allaah (ﷺ) and when they reached us then one of us would lower the Jilbaab upon their faces from her head and then once he had passed, then we would uncover our faces."

The mother of the believers, 'Aa'ishah (رضي الله عنها), is the most complete of the women in terms of religion, knowledge, character, and etiquette. Mustafaa (ﷺ) said concerning her:

> «فَضْلُ عَائِشَةَ عَلَى النِّسَاءِ كَفَضْلِ الثَّرِيدِ عَلَى سَائِرِ الطَّعَامِ»

"The virtue of 'Aa'ishah over women is like the virtue of Thareed over other meals"

Thareed contains meat and bread.

It is affirmed that the Prophet (ﷺ) commanded the women to go out to the Musalla for the 'Eid prayer they said: **"O Messenger of Allaah! One of us does not have a Jilbaab."** The Prophet (ﷺ) said:

> «لِتُلْبِسْهَا أُخْتُهَا مِنْ جِلْبَابِهَا»

"Then let her sister loan her a Jilbaab."[5]

From this narration it is derived that the custom amongst the women of the companions is that the woman would not

---

[5] Reported by Al-Bukhaaree and Muslim

Indecency and Its Dangers | 63

go out of her house except while wearing Jilbaab. The Prophet (ﷺ) did not allow them to go out without wearing Hijaab in order to prevent Fitnah and as a means of protection for them from the causes of corruption and as a means of purification for the hearts of all parties. And this is in spite of the fact that they lived during best generations and the men and the women of that era where from the people of Eemaan and the furthest of the people away from suspicion and doubt.

It is affirmed within the two Saheehs on the authority of 'Aa'ishah (رضي الله عنها), that she said:

«كَانَ رَسُولُ اللَّهِ صلى الله عليه وسلم يُصَلِّي الْفَجْرَ، فَيَشْهَدُ مَعَهُ نِسَاءٌ مِنَ الْمُؤْمِنَاتِ مُتَلَفِّعَاتٍ فِي مُرُوطِهِنَّ ثُمَّ يَرْجِعْنَ إِلَى بُيُوتِهِنَّ مَا يَعْرِفُهُنَّ أَحَدٌ مِنَ الْغَلَسِ»

"The Messenger of Allaah (ﷺ) used to pray the Fajr prayer and the women of the believers would pray along with him covered in their garments and then they would return to their homes and none from amongst the men would recognize them due to the darkness."

This Hadeeth proves that the Hijaab and covering was from the ways of the female companions who are the best of generations and the most noble of them with Allaah, the Might and Majestic. And the loftiest of them in terms of character and manners and the most complete in terms of Eemaan and the most refined of them in terms of their actions. Therefore, they are the righteous example as it relates to their manners and their actions for other than them from those who come after them. Once this is understood, then it becomes clear that that which some of the women do within this time from displaying their adornments and being lax as it relates to the affair of the Hijaab and showing off their beauty to unrelated men and going out into the market places wearing makeup and perfumed is an affair which opposes the legislative evidences and it opposes that which the pious predecessors were upon. It is an affair which is evil.

It is obligatory upon the Muslim rulers, the scholars, and the men who are in charge of the enjoining the good and preventing the evil to change this and to not be silent regarding it. Each one is to work within his capacity and within his capabilities and do that which is able to do utilizing the means which will lead to the prevention of this evil and to make binding upon the women the observance of the Hijaab and proper covering. And the women, they must wear a dress of modesty and dignity and not to crowd with the men within the marketplaces.

From the affairs which are evil that people are recently engaging in within this time is conducting wedding ceremonies in which the wife sits with the groom in the presence of women who are uncovered and showing off their beauty. Perhaps, some of the relatives of the groom attend as well as some the male relatives of the bride. It is not hidden to those who have an upright disposition and religious jealousy that which this action contains from great corruption and the possibility of the strange men to look at the young ladies who are showing off their adornments. Likewise, that which is brought about due to that from evil results. Hence, it is obligatory to prohibit this and to bring it to an end in order to block the means of Fitnah and to safeguard the women from that which opposes the pure legislation.

I advise all of my Muslim brothers within this land and other than it to have Taqwaa of Allaah and to hold fast to His legislation in every regard and to beware of all of that which Allaah has prohibited. Likewise, to stay far away from the means which lead to evil and corruption within marriage ceremonies and other than them; doing so, seeking the Pleasure of Allaah, the Glorified and High, and staying far away from His displeasure and punishment.

I ask Allaah, the Most Generous, to bless us all with following of His Book and clinging to the guidance of His Prophet () and to keep us safe from the affairs which cause deviation in terms of Fitnah and the following of desires and that He show us truth as being the truth and provide us with following it and that He show us falsehood as being falsehood and provide us with the avoidance of it. Indeed, He is the Best of Those Who are Asked. May prayers and peace be upon His servant and messenger, Muhammad, his family, and companions.

✧ ✧ ✧

NOTES

www.ingramcontent.com/pod-product-compliance
Lightning Source LLC
Chambersburg PA
CBHW051715040426
42446CB00008B/901